Constancy.

Friendship.

I love you

Devotion.

Prosperity

Absent but dear.

Truth.

HOPE IS MY STAR.

Have kindly thoughts of me!

Hope dwell in your breast!

When you open this fan
Let it open your heart
To mem'ries that time
In vain bids depart!

FORGET-
ME NOT

Devotion.

Truly

ALBUM
Friendship

Sweet Remembrance